THE CHOICE IS YOURS.

THAT IS THE CORE PHILOSOPHY OF THE MINDFUL LIFE COLLECTION CREATED BY JAE ELLARD. The choice is yours to start anywhere, at any point in your life, to create more awareness around the choices you make each day that either support or sabotage your desired outcome to create meaningful engagement and sustainable balance between the interconnected roles, relationships, and responsibilities that make up your life.

The Mindful Life collection includes four books to generate awareness, reflection, and conversation.

Stop & Think: Creating New Awareness is about the choices you have and your understanding of the impact of those choices.

Stop & See: Developing Intentional Habits is about your ability to consciously choose to create habits that support your definitions of balance and success.

Stop & Listen: Practicing Presence is about working with your choices to create deeper engagement with self, others, and your environment.

Beyond Tips & Tricks: Mindful Management is about leading groups to take accountability for making and accepting choices.

IS IT POSSIBLE TO HAVE BALANCE AND SUCCESS?

That is what this book is about: your ability to consciously choose to create a life that is both balanced and successful through understanding the habits that support or sabotage your desired outcomes.

This book will explore why you do what you do and look at the anatomy of a habit so you can create intentional habits that support your desired outcomes.

BALANCE

LET'S START WITH BALANCE

It doesn't matter what you call balance. You can call it harmony, integration, blur, flexibility, awareness, or another word of your choice. No matter what words you use, the intended outcome is the same: to create easy joy and meaningful engagement between the interconnected relationships, roles, and responsibilities that make up your life.

When it comes to balance, no two people share the same idea or have the same need for balance, because **balance is something different to everyone.**

It's also important to know (and accept) that you will be in and out of balance your entire life as your life shifts and changes.

The meaning of balance changes over time for each person as one's values in life shift with age and through different life experiences.

BALANCE

(Your definition goes here)

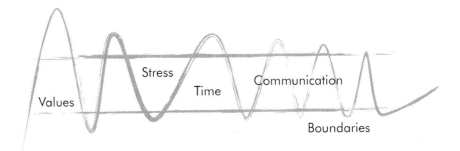

Values   Stress   Time   Communication   Boundaries

Balance is personal, and each person has his or her own idea of what is acceptable, tolerable, and comfortable. It's also very important to remember that there is no right or wrong idea of balance. It is what it is for you and you alone, because you are unique.

The common elements that contribute to or diminish your state of balance include understanding and communicating your values via your words and through your actions, as well as understanding how you use your time and how you respond to stress.

WHAT DOES **BALANCE**
MEAN TO YOU?

I

→ when I feel like I can think
something through end to end and
am able to educate myself along the
way.

→ when I'm eating and using my body
for things other than work

→ no ~~guilt~~ guilt
  ° clear mind
  ° let yourself enjoy it

14

IF YOU HAD **BALANCE,**
WHAT WOULD YOUR LIFE BE LIKE?

Energized

SUCCESS

HOW DOES SUCCESS FIT IN WITH BALANCE?

The other concept that has a tendency to come up when talking about balance is the concept of success. It's no secret that many people around the world feel at times that it is not possible to be successful and have balance at the same time.

The concept of success is very similar to the concept of balance in that, as with balance, success means different things to different people and the definition can change over time as one's life circumstances shift and evolve.

SO WHAT **IS** SUCCESS?

The dictionary defines it as "the favorable or prosperous termination of attempts or endeavors; the accomplishment of one's goals."

Like balance, success has three layers to consider (the same three layers, to be specific):

Individual Success – This is often described and measured by physical, emotional, and spiritual elements (for example, a certain weight, feeling, or state of being).

Personal Success –This is often described and measured in terms of wealth, education, and values (for example, where a person lives, where they went to school, size of family, and social group).

Professional Success – This is often described and measured by recognition, as in a title or salary rank, power and influence, and level of respect received from peers.

Some people have separate definitions of success for each layer. Others have one big idea of success for life.

There is no right or wrong way to define success because it is highly personal, but it is important to know what it means to you as well as what it means to those in your personal and professional life.

A FEELING OR A PERCEPTION?

Also similar to balance is that a definition of success can include both how you want to feel and how you want to be perceived.

For many, success is a combination of both a feeling and a desired perception. Even for those who are on the path to egoless living, on some level there is still a small amount of ego that seeks acknowledgment from someone, somewhere, for something.

Both how you want to feel and how you want to be perceived make up your definition of success.

CONSIDER WHAT IN THIS
MOMENT IS MORE
IMPORTANT TO YOU –
THE WAY YOU FEEL
OR THE WAY YOU ARE
PERCEIVED?

WHAT DOES SUCCESS
MEAN TO YOU RIGHT NOW
IN THIS MOMENT?

No Bullsh*t

Be my own person
and be a model for my
children a.
enabling the success of
my partner.

IF YOU HAD SUCCESS

WHAT WOULD YOUR
LIFE BE LIKE?

HOW DO YOUR VALUES FIT IN?

You values are your most deeply held beliefs that guide the majority of your decisions – where you live, where you work, with whom you live, what you choose for hobbies, and so on.

Your values are the foundation from which you make most choices in life, and having definitions that support them is essential to create sustainable success in your life.

If you are feeling out of balance right now, or feeling that you are not able to achieve the success you desire, it could be that your definitions of balance and success conflict with your values.

Some examples of values include: love, family, friendship, faith, health, wealth, community, compassion, environment, integrity, honesty, freedom, creativity, art, adventure, diversity, accountability, accomplishment, efficiency, calm, loyalty, learning, leadership, innovation, fairness, change, equality, knowledge, cleanliness, flexibility, fun, generosity, orderliness, gratitude, perfection, cooperation, personal growth, perseverance, pleasure, joy, health and well-being, courage, culture, success, thinking, time/timelines, protection, reason, regularity, respect (of self and others), trust, privacy, nature, genius, courtesy, peace . . .

If this is the case for you, don't worry – accept it as an opportunity to revisit what your values are in this moment and validate that your definitions of balance and success are indeed authentic reflections of your current feelings.

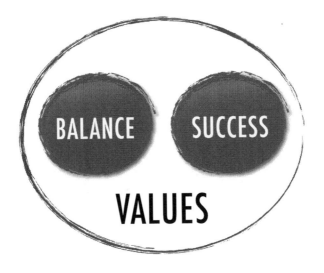

(For some people, this process is ongoing, and it can take time before you find the alignment that feels authentic to you.)

THINK

Ask yourself the following questions:

- What is the relationship between the type of balance you are seeking and your definition of success?

- Are your definitions similar or very different?

- Are they in alignment with your values?

- What is more important to you, balance or success?

- Do balance and success have to be at the expense of each other?

- Is it possible for balance and success to coexist in your life?

DO
Answer the questions.

Share your answers with the important people in your life.

AWARENESS

WHAT DOES AWARENESS HAVE TO DO WITH BALANCE AND SUCCESS?

One solid behavioral trait appears again and again in people who express feeling both success and balance. Those who express feeling balanced and successful have in common **awareness** around when to say no. This awareness then allows people to know how much they can take on and to be able to see their breaking point, before they break.

SO, WHAT DOES
AWARENESS MEAN?

AWARENESS IS THE ABILITY TO **SEE THE WORLD** AND HOW **YOU SHOW UP** IN IT.

It is a deceptively simple concept to understand, and a multilayered skill to develop. This book and the Mindful Life Program are based on the Awareness Framework. The Awareness Framework is built on the idea that behavior has an impact and that there is a result, whether intentional or unintentional, related to the behavior.

When people choose to or are empowered to become more aware of their **behavior**, they are able to be more **accountable** in their roles and to their teams, more authentic in their communication, and more **awake** in their environment (both literally and figuratively).

The impact to the team and organization is a shift in the team's ability to be more **innovative** and more **productive** on multiple levels.

The result is **sustainable success**, both for teams and for individuals.

When you have a framework to begin to understand awareness, you are able to build it as a skill, just like listening or communication.

THE AWARENESS FRAMEWORK

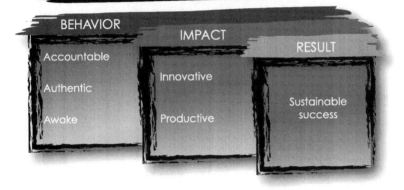

BEHAVIOR

Accountable

Authentic

Awake

IMPACT

Innovative

Productive

RESULT

Sustainable success

AWARENESS AS A SKILL

Awareness — your ability to see the world and how you show up in it — is a skill. Just like learning math, you learn awareness in different layers that build on each other.

First, you have to learn addition and subtraction before you can learn multiplication and division, then you move into algebra, calculus, and statistics. You can't start learning math at a statistics level (well, you can try, but odds are you won't get very far).

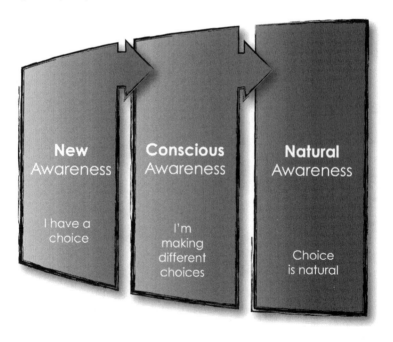

New Awareness

I have a choice

Conscious Awareness

I'm making different choices

Natural Awareness

Choice is natural

New awareness is about taking an inventory of your world and understanding the impact of your behavior on the world around you and within you – things like what makes you happy, sad, and stressed. New awareness is where you become aware you have choices.

Conscious awareness is being more conscious about what it is you are seeing around you and understanding it at a deeper level. It's the place of knowing you have choices. Some days you might make choices that sabotage your desired outcomes for balance and success, and other days you might make choices that support your desired outcomes. Both ways you choose and you are aware that it is a choice.

Natural awareness is where you fully see your behavior patterns and internalize making choices that support your desired outcome for balance and success. This is where balance has become a lifestyle or a habit and feels natural.

WHY IS AWARENESS IMPORTANT?

The skill of awareness is important because it allows you to collect authentic information to help you make informed choices.

Awareness is the ability to collect data with no judgment and no criticism on self or others, just pure observation of what is happening around you and your role in what is happening. You can think of awareness like a little detective inside your head watching you and spying on your inner and outer conversations.

> For example, the voice of awareness might say, "Oh, there I go again, taking my phone into the bedroom at night. Interesting. I'll note that and see if I do it again tomorrow." No judgment, no criticism – just authentic data.

Then, as you develop the skill, your detective becomes more of a bodyguard to help you protect yourself and make informed choices.

For example, awareness as a bodyguard might say, "Okay, self, let's charge your phone in the kitchen before you go to bed. I know you feel out of balance and get stressed first thing in the morning when you see all those messages."

We don't need to see the detective and bodyguard to know they are doing their job – a part of their job is NOT to be seen. Just know they are there and let them do their job, which is to support you in being aware by collecting authentic information to make informed choices that support you in living your values.

Sounds easy, right?

THIS IS WHERE THIS GETS COMPLICATED.

Awareness is the ability (and some might say courage) to see the world and how you show up in it, and action is when you consciously choose to do something about what you see.

EASY: You see it, and you will change it if you don't like it or if it is not supporting you.

NOT SO EASY: Many times we choose not to see, or we see but we choose not to take action.

WHY DO WE SOMETIMES ACT WITHOUT SEEING OR SEE AND CHOOSE NOT TO TAKE ACTION?

HABITS

WHAT IS A HABIT?

Many times, when we choose not to see, or we see but we choose not to take action, it is because of our current habits. Before diving into the anatomy of a habit, it's important to understand what a habit is and to know the difference between a habit and an addiction. It is true that a habit can become an addition, but not all habits are addictions or even close to addiction forming.

A habit is a repeated behavior/action that may be conscious and/or unconscious.

An addiction is continued involvement with an activity or substance despite ongoing negative consequences.

There are two types of addictions to be aware of: a process addiction and chemical addiction.

Process addiction includes things like overeating, gambling, internet, video-gaming, and excessive exercise. For some, work can become a process addiction. People with process addictions are addicted to doing something. It is beyond a habit, because they are unable to stop without assistance or intervention of some kind.

In chemical addiction, the person is unable to alter their habit on their own despite ongoing negative consequences to health, family, and relationships. Examples of this type of addiction include drugs of any kind and alcohol.

As a general rule, you can change a habit on your own, but an addiction may require outside assistance or intervention to change.

GOOD NEWS FOR YOU

Altering a habit or creating a new one to support your desired outcome for balance is not something that requires outside support or intervention. (Support is helpful any time you go through a change, but it is not required to change a habit.)

Most people know that habits can be hard to change. It turns out they are hard to change for many reasons (many of which most of us never learn about), making it even harder to try to create new habits or break old ones.

Habits are incredibly complicated to understand, yet deceptively simple to create and change. This only occurs once you have context around the anatomy of a habit and have developed the skill of awareness to see your habits clearly.

There is a wealth of information available on the topic of habits. Several professions study habits, each in unique ways. Some of the key disciplines that study habits include:

* behavioral science
* psychology
* sociology
* addiction medicine
* neuroscience
* marketing
* advertising

With so many experts around the world studying habits, there is a LOT of data on why we do what we do and how habits impact society, economies, systems, and relationships with others and ourselves. For example, marketers know that 80%-90% of purchasing decisions are rooted in habit.

SO HOW CAN THIS DATA HELP YOU CREATE MORE BALANCE IN YOUR LIFE?

Well, researchers also know that up to **90% of everyday behavior is based on habits**. That's right – it means almost everything we do each day is based on habit, which means that creating balance in your life can be as simple as creating a balance habit.

Ninety percent is a huge percentage, and it is important that you know not all habits are bad; in fact, habits are great for humans. (This is great news if almost everything we do is based on habit!)

Science tells us that humans develop habits to save effort and conserve energy. The brain will try to make most anything a habitual pattern to give us more mental bandwidth and energy to do other things that cannot become a habit.

So that means that each day, our brains look for patterns in our actions that can be turned into a habit. This allows you to automate that action (or "power down" your brain) while doing that action and apply the energy saved to other actions that are not habits, such as creating a strategy, writing a review, or having a meaningful conversation.

PHYSIOLOGY OF A HABIT

Sometimes when we create a certain habit, our bodies create an associated chemical reaction to correlate to that habit. Over time it is possible (depending on the habit) to get hooked on the chemical link or reward associated with certain habits.

For example, the habit of being a people pleaser creates dopamine in the brain – a chemical that makes us feel good. So when you help people, you feel good – which is great, unless it's a habit that is preventing you from helping yourself first when needed and appropriate.

So at times when we change our behavior to develop a new habit, it's both an external and internal change for our bodies.

Now it begins to make sense why changing a habit feels uncomfortable: because it literally feels different in the body as different chemicals are created with the creation of a new habit.

In the example of being a people pleaser, when you start to say no more often to requests, your body will at first miss the dopamine it was used to receiving as the reward for helping people. This is a desire that will dissolve over a short period of time, as the body adapts quickly to internal changes such as these.

YOU CANNOT ELIMINATE A HABIT

That's right – you cannot eliminate a habit, only replace it. This is because once a habit is created, there is an associated neural pathway that stays in the brain forever correlated to that habitual pattern. So what happens in overly simple terms is when you alter a habit, you change what is flowing in the pathway.

Think of it like a highway, with the old habit being a car driving on the road and the creation of a new habit being a different car entering the same highway.

To change what is flowing in the pathway, it's a simple three-step process, one that many experts call the "habit loop."

TO CHANGE WHAT IS
    FLOWING IN THE PATHWAY,
**IT'S A SIMPLE
    THREE-STEP
PROCESS.**

THE HABIT LOOP

The habit loop is made up of a **cue**, followed by a routine **behavior**, then a **reward**.

A cue, also called a trigger, can be things like physical location, time of day, emotional feeling, or a person or group of persons, preceding an action such as waking up, entering the office in the morning, or going home after work. A reward is why you do what you do: it can be a feeling, a perception, or a goal.

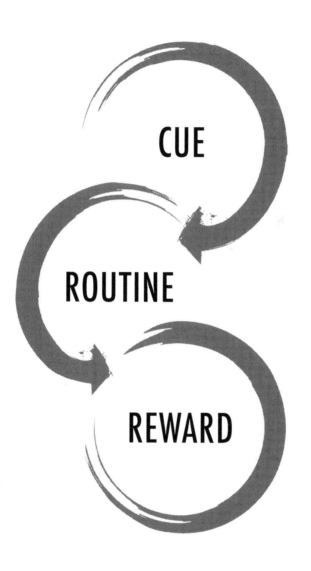

THREE STEPS TO MODIFY A HABIT

Before you can create a new habit, you have to determine WHY you have created this habit in the first place – what is motivating your choice. In other words, you need to understand the reward you are seeking or receiving from doing what you do. That way you can create a routine that address the desired reward or outcome you are seeking.

The first step toward creating a new habit or replacing an existing habit is to change your routine.

This is where the skill of **AWARENESS** comes in. Replacing a routine requires awareness – your ability to see the world and how you show up in it.

If you lack awareness around your behavior (routines), it will be really difficult to change or create a new habit.

Next, repetition of routine becomes key. On average, it will take about 60 days to create a new habit (although it could take as few as 20 days or as many as 300 days). The key is that the new routine must map to the true reward, then be repeated enough times so the brain can see the pattern.

If only that were enough to create a new habit, so many people wouldn't be stuck in old habits that might sabotage their desired outcomes.

The two next steps that are needed to ensure a behavior change includes a **belief that it is possible** to create or alter the intended habit, which is linked with having that belief supported by a group.

So you have to believe you can really do it and then share that belief with others – this could be your friends, family, co-workers, or people in a chat room, Meetup, or an organized club. It doesn't matter who, it just matters that you believe you can do it and that others support you in that belief.

Some researchers say it is essential that the belief the habit can be altered is supported by a group. This is the foundation for 12-step programs like Alcoholic Anonymous and all of the other related Anonymous programs, as well as weight loss programs like Weight Watchers and Jenny Craig. Group training fitness models as well as entire social movements are also based on this same idea.

That's right – entire social movements also follow this model (for example, civil rights, gay rights, and women's rights). Both of these social movements follow the same model at a group level: a desire to change behavior and a belief it is possible, supported by a community of people who in most cases don't even know one another.

WHAT DO HABITS HAVE TO DO WITH BALANCE?

If 90% of behavior is based on habits, it safe to assume that habits are intimately related to supporting or sabotaging desired outcomes for balance and success.

It's possible that creating balance in your life could be as simple as creating a habit to support your definition of balance.

That's right – creating balance could be as simple as creating a habit to support what balance means for you.

> For example, if balance means having deeper engagement, you could alter your habit of multitasking, or if balance means having more time to "think" without interruption, you could create a habit to block off time each day in your calendar to just think.

Habits are the way in which we create the life we want to have, and our habits either support balance as a lifestyle choice or not.

When it comes to these balance-supporting habits, there are not many role models within corporate hierarchies actively practicing and promoting balance habits and choosing balance as a lifestyle.

This is because the global corporate landscape has not accepted balance habits as a behavioral norm … **YET.**

What is so exciting is that there are thousands, hundreds of thousands, if not millions of people in the world who share the belief that is possible to be successful AND balanced and have some really good ideas on how to do it. Their ideas can become habits, and these habits can transform the way people work.

Right now there are people working together without even knowing each other, creating a new way of work in which it is possible to create a habit for balance and that supports success.

It really has only been in the last decade that companies were even willing to talk about work-life balance, let alone offer frameworks and tools to help employees achieve it and opportunities to openly discuss the challenges.

Because you are reading this, you are at the beginning of a huge shift in corporate consciousness, a huge shift in how people relate to work, a shift in creating a habit of balance.

Based on the very fact you are reading this, you are part of a movement that is going to change the habits of working professionals for generations to come. And the way to do this is one habit – one **balance** habit – at a time.

You know what balance and success mean to you.

You know what awareness is.

You know how to alter or create a new habit.

The only thing left to do is to create an intentional habit to support your idea of balance.

The one habit I'm willing to create or replace that will support my definitions of balance and success is:

NEW HABIT (Routine)

Dedicate at least one night together with <u>no technology</u> - no <u>TV</u>.

CUE (What will remind me to do this new habit?)

Calender. Support from Kevin

POST ITS.

REWARD (Current and/or new)

Continued learning and quality time.

(Plus meditation earlier in the day.

What will you do when you feel blocked from doing your
new habit?

Remind myself f the
long view. Re-prioritize.
meditate or deep breaths.

Right now in this moment, you have the ability to consciously choose to create a life that meets your aspirations for balance and success. For each person the choices will be different, because balance and success mean different things to different people.

You now have an understanding of what a habit is (and isn't) and the context to know how habits help support you and sometimes sabotage your desired outcomes.

With this information, you can choose to create intentional habits that support your desired outcomes. Just like with creating any type of habit, creating a habit for balance starts with awareness – your ability to see the world and how you show up in it – so you can use that information to make intentional choices.

For some the journey may be short, only a couple of weeks to create a lasting habit. For others the journey may take a year or longer as your awareness deepens to create new habits.

If you truly desire to make balance a lifestyle, what matters most is just beginning the journey – there is no right or wrong place to start.

THE CHOICE IS YOURS.

MINDFUL THOUGHTS...

MINDFUL THOUGHTS...

MINDFUL THOUGHTS...

MINDFUL THOUGHTS...

MINDFUL THOUGHTS...

MINDLESS THOUGHTS...

ABOUT THE AUTHOR

After years in senior communication roles, working countless hours crafting content for executives at Microsoft, Jae collapsed from stress-related adrenal fatigue directly attributed to the way she was living her life. This life-altering experience propelled Jae deep into research on human behavior, neuroscience, mindfulness, and organizational relationship systems.

In 2008, Jae founded WLB Consulting Group and developed the Mindful Life Program, which includes four group coaching workshops to generate reflection, awareness, and action at the organizational and individual levels.

Jae has taught work-life awareness workshops to thousands of employees at Microsoft and other technology companies in more than 50 countries including China, Russia, India, Japan, Brazil, Argentina, United Arab Emirates, France, Germany, United Kingdom, Norway, Sweden, Canada, and the United States.

Jae has an extensive background in writing and communication with a master's degree in Communication Management from Colorado State University and a bachelor's degree in Broadcast Communication from Metropolitan State College of Denver. She holds certificates in co-active coaching and organizational relationship systems coaching and is the author of seven books.

OTHER BOOKS BY JAE ELLARD

The Five Truths about Work-life Balance is about moving past the misconceptions surrounding work, life, and balance.

The Pocket Coach: Perspective When You Need Some is a book of questions to help you make clear choices.

Success with Stress is about five proactive choices you can make to reduce stress.

THE MINDFUL LIFE COLLECTION

Stop & Think: Creating New Awareness is about the choices you have and the understanding of the impact of the choices you make.

Stop & See: Developing Intentional Habits is about your ability to consciously choose to create habits that support your definitions of balance and success.

Stop & Listen: Practicing Presence is about working with your choices to create deeper engagement with self, others and your environment.

Beyond Tips & Tricks: Mindful Management is about leading groups to take accountability for making and accepting choices.

Created by Jae Ellard

Edited by Jenifer Kooiman

Designed by Hannah Wygal

Stop and See: Mindful Management, 1st edition

2011-2014 Copyright by Simple Intentions

ISBN 978-0-9828344-8-0

Simple Intentions is a conscious content company working to increase awareness in the workplace. For more information please visit www.simpleintentions.com.

47047790R00058

Made in the USA
Charleston, SC
27 September 2015